HANDS-ON CELEBRATIONS

ART ACTIVITIES FOR ALL AGES

Palmer Public Library
655 S. Valley Way
Palmer, Alaska 99645

W9-BRJ-554

Can you find the jaguar head mask, the beaded snakes, the flute, the circle of clay figures

FOLK ART OF CENTRAL & SOUTH AMERICA

Throughout Central and South America there is a mix of Spanish and pre-Columbian influences. The culture, religion and folk art is a blend that is both unique and identifiable. The native cultures have retained their original forms and continue to present them with contemporary adaptations especially for celebrations.

...hat are part of a whistle, the clay mask, and the wooden carved jaguar?

This book is dedicated to my mother, Wilma Hanson Young,
who continues to celebrate each day.

Book design and photography by
Art and International Productions
Graphic Design by Jennifer Moody and Jim Tilly
Photography by Sasha Sagan

Some of the art activities were drawn, designed and student-tested by
Jody Jenkins and Shala Dobson, art instructors.

Mary Simpson illustrated the calendar pages.

Copyright © Yvonne Young Merrill

First paperback printing: October 1995
Printed in Hong Kong

Published and distributed by K/ITS
2359 East Bryan Avenue
Salt Lake City, Utah 84108

Library of Congress
Card Catalog Number: 95-79085

ISBN 0 - 9643177 - 4 - 5

All rights reserved. No part of this book may be reproduced or utilized in any
form or by any means, electronic or mechanical, including photocopying,
recording or by any information storage and retrieval system,
without permission in writing from the publisher.

HANDS-ON CELEBRATIONS

ART ACTIVITIES FOR ALL AGES

YVONNE Y. MERRILL

PUBLISHED BY K/ITS • ANCHORAGE, ALASKA

CONTENTS

INTRODUCTION

CELEBRATIONS have been happening since the dawn of civilization. Early man's ritual was concerned with **survival**: the hunt, the fertility of the earth, the rain, the harvest, the sun. All are forces that he saw as controlling life. Fear of hunger evolved into elaborate sacrifices, dances, art, and events which were meant to appease Earth Forces. Fear of darkness made **fire** and **light** elements worthy of beckoning forth; rejoicing occured when they reappeared. Fear of bad luck, illness and death brought about symbols of power in the forms of tattoos and body adornment such as face painting. Art as imagery, masks, and shrines prevailed as spectacular forms of magic.

Growing up involved universal Celebrations with the birth of a child, passing into adolescence, the event of marriage, the achievement of status, and death. These are all rich in traditional ritual, clothing, foods, gift giving, and objects. Common themes in worldwide Celebrations recur and are easily recognized.

These themes prevail in our Celebration story:

Earth Theme: Dependency on the bounty of the earth has brought about planting festivals, objects encouraging the fertility of the earth and all living things, success of the harvest and the final joy of the feast.

Air Theme: Atmospheric launching of balloons and rockets, firecrackers, incense, banners, kites, flags and pennants are part of Celebrations.

Fire Theme: Firecrackers, the glow of candles, flaming bonfires, burning straw and paper figures, lanterns and torches all symbolize the essential light of the sun.

Water Theme: Floating, dousing, dunking and showering with water are symbolic of cleansing and purification.

These primary themes are supported with music and song, costuming and jewelry, face and body painting, shrines and altars, dramatics with props and masks, dancing, games, color and special foods. Each element contributes to the spirit of the Celebration.

All people have Celebrations. Sometimes one of these occasions is called a Holiday from the English word "Haligdaeg" (holy day).

Holidays were recorded in the calendar according to the moon, sun, stars and seasons.

HOW TO USE THIS BOOK

This book features 26 celebrations from 16 countries. The full color photographs of crafts clearly present the products you will create. Simple drawings and instructions make it easy to do the activities.

The celebration projects are enrichments for:

- party themes
- gift ideas
- simple costumes that are completions for a mask or hat
- multicultural school and community events
- projects for family enrichment
- ideas for activities when teaching a multicultural unit
- art fun for community fairs
- entertaining children on a rainy day with a wholesome and productive craft

Games, recipes, props, costumes and gifts enhance festivals practiced around the world. Many social and community occasions are made memorable by a hand made prop bearing authenticity. Whether you or others create it – the addition of the craft might help create a memory.

The look of the book
Each set of four months is introduced by an overview of celebrations in many parts of the world. This section is also introduced by a photograph of folk crafts from a global region. These object-filled pictures have a seek-and-find game that challenges you to find a specific item. The answer key in the back of the book identifies the items and explains something about them.

Getting started
- Put newspaper or plastic on your work surface to protect it from messes
- Wear a coverup —an old shirt, apron or garbage bag with neck and arm holes
- Have a grown-up help with scissors, knife cutting or hot glue guns
- Read all the instructions before you start
- When you have finished, tidy up. Put tops on paints and glue. Empty and clean water containers. Take good care of brushes by washing them in soapy water and rinsing them thoroughly.

Craft tools

Every effort has been made to use accessible, inexpensive, safe tools and materials for the projects in this book. Our decorating tools are common to most households, schools and community programs. They include:

- Wax crayons
- Washable and sometimes permanent markers
- Oil pastels
- Washable acrylic paint
- Tempera paint
- A watercolor brush with a small tip
- A utility knife (adult supervision is recommended)
- A hot-glue or craft gun (handy, but this tool gets dangerously hot and should only be used with adult supervision)

Materials

We have tried to produce nearly all activities with paper. We rely on:

- posterboard, available in most supermarkets
- file folders, which you may be discarding
- construction paper, available in packets of many colors
- butcher paper, which comes on large rolls and is now available in art and school supply stores, copy stores, and in all schools
- plain newsprint, inexpensive and available from most printing companies
- tissue paper, crepe paper and paper plates

We encourage you to use everyday, throwaway items. This saves you money and recycles potentially useful items that could stimulate creativity.

Use your imagination when choosing materials. If you don't have a paint tray, use a paper plate, pie tin or foil-covered pan (if you cover the pan with foil, paint cleanup is easier).

Preparing a hollowed egg:

Hollowed eggs are used for two activities in the book. You will find them on pages 30 and 36.
1. Eggs must be raw and at room temperature if possible.
2. Have paper towels or dish cloths ready for gentle gripping.
3. Using a needle, scissors point, or pencil point, gently prick the narrow end of the egg and make a small hole.
4. At the other end of the egg make another hole a little larger than a pencil eraser. You are going to blow the insides of the egg through the larger hole.
5. To break up the yolk before you blow, stick a toothpick or skewer into the larger hole and gently push it through the yolk and loosen it.
6. Put your mouth to the smallest hole and blow the white and yolk through the large hole. It takes a little time and you have to be careful not to break the shell.
7. Wash off the inside and outside of the egg and let it drain and dry overnight.

Can you find the winged flying figure, the wooden puppet, some beautiful fabrics, a puppet

FOLK ART FROM BALI

Bali is known for its excellence in crafts. Folk art has always been essential to Bali. The most revered member of the community was the craftsman and the highest status was saved for the preserver and presenter of the puppets. Textiles, woodworking, painting, metalwork and forms from nature are abundant and basic to Balinese folk art.

JANUARY

January hails the New Year in most cultures. New beginnings for everyone mark January, the first month in the New Year.

New Year's Day in Scotland is called **HOGMANAY**. "First footing" or the first person to set foot over the threshold symbolizes the year's luck.

SHOOGATSU is celebrated by the Japanese and involves thorough house cleaning and decorating the front door with good luck rice-straw ropes, pine boughs and bamboo. Red and white ribbons decorate the household broom.

In Ecuador **ANO VIEGO** (Old Year), a straw figure, is dressed in wornout clothes. The family faults are written on paper scraps and pinned to the figure. At a certain moment the straw man is burned, starting the New Year with a clean slate.

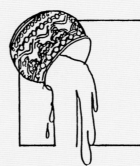

CHAING MAI in Thailand features a symbolic dousing for purification for the New Year.

In Greece, a **NEW YEAR** cake is baked called a peta after the coin that is baked into it. You guessed it—whoever finds the coin gets the luck for the coming year.

FEBRUARY

February is a month rich in a variety of celebrations: famous birthdays, paper tokens of love, costumed paraders, sled dog races and flower festivals.

FUR RENDEZVOUS is the most popular celebration in Alaska, used to be a gathering time for trappers. Fur auctions, Eskimo blanket tosses, feasting and dances were held. Today Fur "Rondy" is a ten-day event with a Miners and Trappers Ball, carnivals, snow sculptures and displays. The final event of Anchorage's celebration is the World Championship sled dog race.

GROUNDHOG DAY on February 2 involved weather watching for German farmers who carefully noted hibernating animals as signs of weather predictions. The badger's emergence in the Old World was replaced with the more plentiful ground hog in the New World. If the groundhog saw his shadow there were to be six more weeks of winter. If the day was cloudy and shadow-free, spring was soon to come.

PRESIDENT'S DAY includes Lincoln's birthday on February 12 and honors the sixteenth president— known for his leadership, wisdom, industry, humor and honesty. Washington's birthday is February 22 and recognizes the "Father of his Country". He is known as the president who was "first in war, first in peace and first in the hearts of his countrymen." In 1789 he was elected the first President and served two terms.

CANDLEMAS on February 2, was an ancient Roman candle procession honoring Persephone, the goddess of Spring. Christianity adopted the holiday and the candles decorated the Virgin Mary's altar. Because it was mid-winter, everyone yearned for spring and the light of the candle symbolized its advent. On Candlemas Day in France people make crepes while holding something gold in their hand for good luck. It was said, "If Candlemas was fair and clear, there would be two winters in the year."

March is thought of as the windy month to welcome longed-for spring. The wearing of the green on St. Patrick's Day honors Ireland's patron saint. March is the month the sun crosses the celestial equator (the Vernal Equinox) and marks March 21 the first day of spring.

March 1 is a national holiday in Wales called **ST. DAVID'S DAY**. Patriotic Welsh men and women wear a leek, the national plant which resembles an over-sized onion. Centuries ago the tiny country was invaded, and fighting Welshmen were meeting their defeat. Part of the tactical problem seemed to be that friend and foe were impossible to identify. The young monk David pulled a leek from a nearby garden and recommended that the Welshmen thrust one under their headgear. They did and were victorious. Ever since, the lowly leek has been a March vegetable of honor in Wales.

HOLI: a celebration of the Festival of Spring. It is characterized by bright random splashes and splotches of vivid color. The Holi celebration lasts from three to ten days and finds revelers spraying colored water, throwing pigmented powder and dunking unsuspecting victims. People have symbolic bonfires to burn away winter and frighten evil spirits. Different regions celebrate Holi in a variety of ways: tall poles or effigies may be burned, some areas have fairs with booths and carnivals and some have parades with young people throwing colored water and powder at the crowd.

HINA MATSURI, March 3, is Girl's Doll Festival day for youngsters in Japan. It is a day for displaying heirloom doll collections, wearing a traditional kimono, sharing dolls and enjoying the traditional tea ceremony with other girls. Fresh blossoms garland the doll displays. Stores and commercial places often display dolls on this day.

March 25 is the **GREEK NATIONAL HOLIDAY**. Blue and white flags fly from every house and the national anthem is played. People wear their national costume and dance the traditional Greek folk dances.

April is rich in celebrations, many of which center on seasonal change. The anticipation of planting has always involved rain festivals, fertility of the soil beliefs, and renewed growth. Christians celebrate death and resurrection at Easter and Jews the passing over of death's angel centuries ago in Egypt.

PASSOVER, one of the most important Jewish holidays, is celebrated for eight days in March or April. By 1300 B.C. the Jews had been slaves for 210 years in Egypt. Passover is the holiday for independence which marks the exodus of the Jews from Egypt under the leadership of Moses. Special dinners are held called "Seders". It is believed that God sent an angel of death to kill the first-born of all families. The Jews were told to mark their houses and the angel would "pass over" them.

Thailand's Water Festival is a joyous welcome to spring. Called **SONGKRAN** the three-day celebration begins the Buddhist New Year. Water is thrown playfully, but the sprinkling of water is a form of a blessing. The act of freedom is emphasized by freeing caged birds and releasing pet fish into natural streams. Songkran finds Thais dressed in flowers, dancing traditional Thai dances and electing a local queen to reign over the festivals.

The first day of April has been an **ALL FOOLS' DAY** for many cultures. The Romans believed that Ceres was on a fool's errand as she searched for her daughter Proserpina. Some trace April Fools' Day to 1564 when the news of a calender change was slow to travel. New Year's Day changed from April 1 to January 1, but some "fools" continued to celebrate in April.

BUDDHA'S BIRTHDAY is April 8. Altars in shrines and homes are decorated with flowers, food, candles and incense. Tea is poured over the statue's head, symbolic of Buddha's miracle of changing water to tea.

LI SEE ENVELOPES & ORNAMENT

LI SEE ENVELOPES
A CHINESE NEW YEAR GIFT FOR CHILDREN

Materials: red construction paper cut into 6" squares, gold paint, glitter, glue, markers, crayons, paper scraps.

1. Make a good luck wish for a friend on one side of the red construction paper. You may use markers, crayons, paint or glitter. Let dry.

2. Turn over and fold up 1 corner about 1".

3. Fold corner up again.

4. Fold each side corner to the middle, overlapping slightly. Glue or tape in place.

5. Fold the top corner down and tuck into place.

6. Before giving the envelope to a friend add a small coin, a wise quote or a good luck message.

The **Chinese New Year** pops with firecrackers, glows with lanterns and brims with special foods—not for a day but for nearly a month. It falls on the first day of the new moon between January 21 and February 20. Not only is this the New Year but it is also the traditional birthday for all Chinese. No matter when a baby is born in the previous year, he is considered to be exactly one year old on New Year's Day.

ORNAMENT

A CHINESE NEW YEAR DECORATION

Materials: scissors, glue or glue stick, markers, watercolors or crayons, a copy of the pattern.

1. Cut out the polyhedron forms.

2. Decorate with crayons, markers or watercolors.

3. Fold on each dotted line. Also fold under each tab.

4. Begin construction by gluing Tab A under Edge A.

5. Work slowly and let dry carefully before moving on to a new glue tab.

Think about New Year's decorations or symbols with which you can decorate your ornament: a hat, a noisemaker, a horn, a clock.

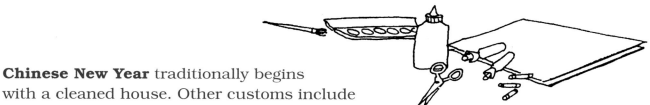

Chinese New Year traditionally begins with a cleaned house. Other customs include hiding all sharp objects, painting the gate bright red, and gathering red chopsticks and red candles—the redder, the luckier. A red seal is placed on the door at midnight as well as a red scroll wishing passersby a Happy New Year. Yellow chrysanthemums and red hibiscus blossoms are displayed along with the "money tree" heavy with gold coins, tied-on wishes, paper flowers and red "li see" envelopes.

USE THE PATTERNS ON THE OPPOSITE PAGE TO HELP CONSTRUCT YOUR ORNAMENT.

PATTERNS

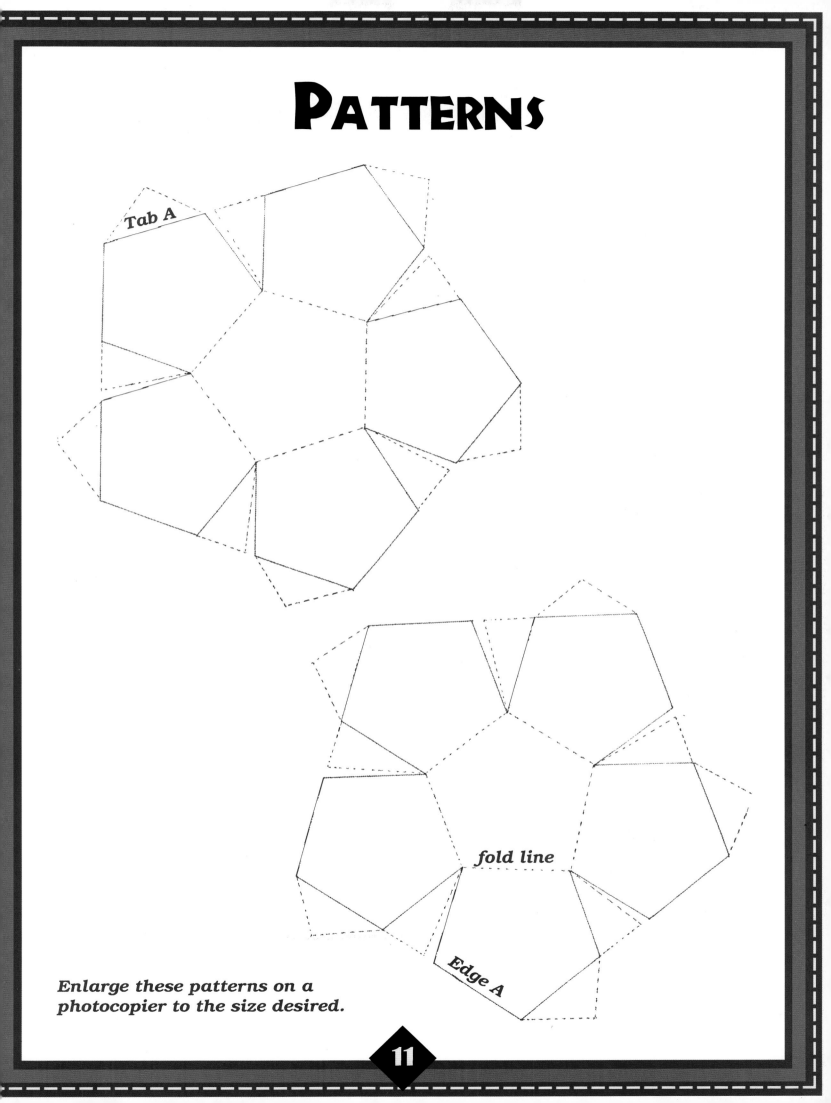

Tab A

fold line

Edge A

*Enlarge these patterns on a
photocopier to the size desired.*

WAITANGI DAY

WAITANGI DAY CANOE

MAORI SYMBOLS ON A PAPER BOAT

Materials: 4 sheets of 9" x 18" brown construction paper, glue, scissors, a black marker.

1. Glue 2 pieces of brown paper together. Do the same to the other 2 pieces of paper. (This will make the canoe extra strong).

2. Draw the shape of your canoe on one of the glued brown papers. Cut it out. Trace the cutout on the other piece of brown paper. Now you have 2 sides for your canoe. Save the scraps to cut out the bottom of the canoe.

3. Decorate both sides of the canoe with patterns or symbols. You may use Maori symbols or make up your own. Use a black marker to decorate your canoe.

4. Glue the ends of the canoe together. Do not glue the middle where the arrows are pointing. This part must be left open to make the bottom of the canoe. Let dry.

5. Put the canoe down on the leftover brown paper and trace around the bottom of the canoe. Put glue on the traced line. Set the canoe on the glue. Hold in place and let it dry. Cut off the excess paper leaving only the bottom of the canoe. To make a seat for your canoe cut a strip 1" x 2 1/2" and glue it in place.

On February 6, **New Zealand** celebrates the 1840 Treaty that the **Maoris** made with the British when the Great Fleet of seven carved canoes landed in New Zealand. "Waka" means canoe in Maori culture. They made their beautifully carved boats from wood and used symbols important to them. The shape of the hills is in the flowing lines, the shapes of trees and ferns in the curling fronds and spirals. You can make your canoe out of paper and use symbols important to you to decorate it.

Mardi Gras Mask

Mardi Gras Mask

A Costume & Mask Holiday

Materials: assorted paper scraps, construction paper 4" x 8" (you may use thin tag board, railroad board or cardboard for a stronger base), tissue paper and wallpaper scraps, glitter, felt, string, pipe cleaners, found objects (such as feathers, buttons, sequins), glue, scissors, markers, crayons, masking tape, hole punch.

1. Hold the 4" x 8" construction paper up to your eyes. With a crayon mark approximately where your eye holes are. (Have a partner help you). Cut out the eye holes in any shape.

2. Cut along the edge of your mask creating an interesting shape. Cut a small place where your nose will be.

3. Punch out a hole on both sides for the string that holds your mask. Reinforce the holes as well as the entire back of your mask with masking tape strips.

4. Decorate your mask with markers, feathers, crayons, glitter or any found objects. Traditional colors are gold, green and purple.

Mardi Gras, the last day before Lent, means Fat Tuesday in French. A fat ox was paraded down the streets of Paris to remind people not to eat meat during Lent. Lent is a forty-day period of fasting and self denial in preparation for Easter in the Christian world. Just before Lent, people wear costumes and elaborate masks to balls and parades. There is often royalty elected for the occasion. The French brought the celebration to Louisiana, and New Orleans hosts the most famous American Mardi Gras. It was first held in 1704.

WOVEN HEART BASKETS

WOVEN HEART BASKET

A VARIATION ON A DANISH CHRISTMAS ORNAMENT

Materials: construction paper 4" x 12" (2 sheets per person, preferably white, light pink or red), pencil, scissors, glue, ruler, markers (fine tip red or black).

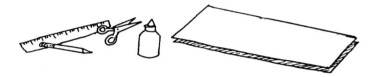

1. Fold each 4" x 12" construction paper sheet in half lengthwise.

2. Measure 4" up from the fold on each paper and lightly draw a straight line.

3. Round off the top edges with a light pencil line and cut them.

4. Cut from the middle of the fold up to the pencil line on both papers.

5. Weave both papers together by sliding one flap gently through the doubled paper. You want to create an open basket. (This part is tricky).

6.   Add a 4-6 " strip for a handle. To make a more complicated and interesting woven valentine, make several cuts from the bottom as shown in step 6.

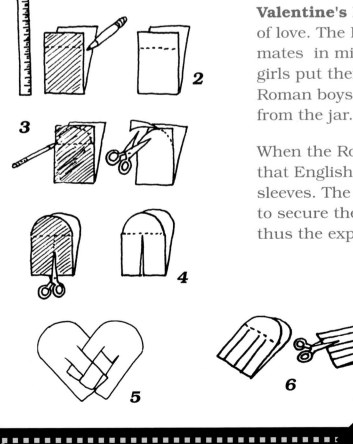

Valentine's Day is February 14, a special day for sentiments of love. The Romans believed animals and birds chose their mates in mid-February. On this day unmarried Roman girls put their names on a slip of paper in a jar. The single Roman boys chose the name of their "sweetheart" from the jar.

When the Roman army invaded the British Isles they found that English men often attached a token of their love to their sleeves. The Roman boys liked this idea so much they began to secure the names of their sweethearts to their sleeves—thus the expression "wearing your heart on your sleeve".

FOLK ART FROM RUSSIA

Russian crafts have flourished for centuries. A nesting doll painter has had years of special art training, completed work as an apprentice and makes a living at their craft. The artist that creates folk art has the same status as any professional. Crafts are regional and often an important economic base for communities. Some areas are experts in the birch bark industry and some in fine porcelain and glaze work. The crafts presented here represent those that are typically available today.

Can you find the small to large nesting dolls, the doll that covers a tea pot, containers fancy eggs and a patterned shawl typical of Russia? Answers on page 79.

made from birch bark, metal hot water holders called samovars, a very old book, several

HAMMERED SHAMROCK LEAF PRINTS

HAMMERED SHAMROCK LEAF PRINTS

A St. Patrick's Day fabric print using a shamrock plant

Materials: a healthy, full shamrock plant, a hammer or pounder, 100% cotton fabric, washing soda available at the supermarket, protective papers, brush, soapy water, ink-free newsprint.

1. Find a sturdy, flat surface and cover it with newspaper. Place ink-free newsprint on top. Lay some cotton scraps on top of the paper. Carefully place the shamrock leaves face down on the fabric.

2. Put several pieces of ink-free newsprint on top of the leaves and fabric. Pound with a hammer where you judge the leaves are. Carefully lift a corner of your paper to check the printing.

3. After pounding the leaves, dip your fabric into a solution of 2 tablespoons washing soda and 3 cups water. What happened to your leaf print? Did it turn a new color?

4. Wash and dry the fabric.

5. You are now ready to make a shamrock project. Consider using napkins, a handkerchief or scarf, etc. Repeat steps 1-3.

St. Patrick's Day honors the patron Saint of Ireland. On March 17, loyal Irishmen wear green shamrocks, drink green beverages and eat Irish soda bread. Many cities have parades and everyone wishes each other Good Luck! St. Patrick lived around the year 400 A.D. It is believed he was born in Britain but was captured by pirates at the age of sixteen and sold as a slave in Ireland. He escaped six years later but returned to teach the people Christianity and how to read and write.

PURIM GROGGER

Purim Grogger

A Jewish children's noisemaker

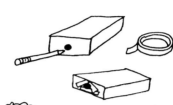

Materials: small cereal or gelatin boxes (1 per person), dried beans or grains, tempera paint, stick (wooden dowel, or a long pencil at least 12" long, 1 per box), masking tape. If you do not have tempera paint you could always use cut paper, glue, markers or crayons.

1. Carefully punch a hole in the top and bottom of your cereal box with a sharp pencil or scissors. Reinforce both holes with masking tape.

2. Put a small number of dried beans into the hole in the box to make the grogger's noise.

3. With tempera paint and small brushes paint the box. To help the paint adhere to the surface of the box add 1 tablespoon of liquid dishwashing detergent to 1/2 cup of paint.

4. When the box is dry, insert the wooden dowel through both holes. Do not glue into place. The box should move freely around the stick. You may have to enlarge the holes in your box slightly.

5. To use your grogger hold one end of the stick and make quick circular motions with your hand. The box should spin round and round the middle of the stick creating quite a noise with the beans inside.

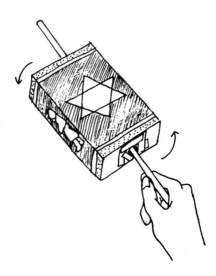

Purim (Poor'im), the Festival of Lots, is celebrated in March by Jews all over the world. It is as eagerly anticipated by Jewish children as Christmas is by Christian young people. Purim celebrates the Old Testament story of Haman, a wicked advisor to the king who wanted to kill all Jews in Persia. To decide on which day the killings should take place "lots" were drawn. The festival celebrates the saving of the Jews by Esther and Mordecai. A special cookie basket is made, the shalot manst is filled with triangle-shaped cookies called Hamentashen and given to special friends. The grogger is part of a dramatic presentation traditionally performed by family members.

JAPANESE PAPER DOLLS

JAPANESE PAPER DOLLS
FOR EVERYONE TO DO AT HINA MATSURI

Materials: colored copy paper or origami patterned paper (1/2 sheet, 5 1/2" x 8 1/2"), scissors, glue, markers, paper scraps.

1. Cut your sheet of paper in half as shown.

2. Cut a small head shape about the size of a quarter with a long neck from a scrap piece of paper. Draw facial features with a pencil. Save until later.

3. A) Take one of your pieces of paper. Cut 1/2" strip off the long edge.
   B) Fold the top edge of this paper over twice.
   C) Turn this over so that the folds are on the back. Locate the center and fold both top corners to the center as shown making the neckline of the kimono. Leave a small space in the neckline to hold your head shape.
   D) Fold each side in again, lining up the bottom edges as you fold. If one side sticks out simply cut it off.

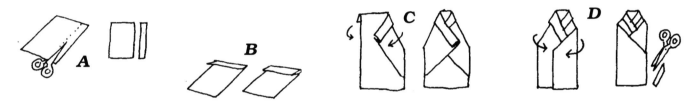

4. Take the 1/2" strip from step 3 and wrap it around the waist beginning in the front. Either glue or fold under in the back. Insert the head.

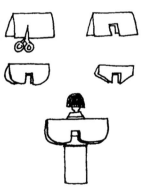

5. Next take another sheet of paper to make the sleeves. Cut off a 1" strip from the short edge. Fold the larger piece in half. Cut a rectangle into the center of the open edges (no larger than kimono form). Round off each edge for a girl's kimono or cut off angular straight sleeves for a boy's. Glue onto back of kimono with open slit down.

6. Fold a 1" strip into an obi sash for the back if you wish. Try any fancy fold you like.

Hina Matsuri is Japanese Girl's Day in Japan and is also Doll Festival Day. It is a holiday when parents express their love and pride in their daughters.

During **Hina Matsuri** girls wear their best kimonos and hold a tea ceremony with invited girls and their dolls. All are very polite and have proper manners as they enjoy the sweet rice cakes in colors of green, pink and white.

FOOL'S HAT

FOOL'S HAT

A HAT FOR THE GERMAN FASCHING KARNEVAL

Materials: red and white construction paper 18" x 24", gold or silver glitter, tempera paint (red, white, gold, silver, and black), markers, scissors, glue, masking tape, stapler.

1. Fold the 18" x 24" sheet of red or white construction paper in half the long way as shown. Then fold it again in half the long way.

2. Bring both ends together and staple to fit your head. This is the base of your Fool's Hat.

3. With red and white construction paper cut out a variety of large and small curled shapes.

4. Choose certain shapes that you like and insert into the folds of the circular form you made. Try several kinds of shapes.

5. It is good to use at least 2 large shapes on opposite sides of your hat. Glue these together at the top to create the crest for your hat.

6. Glue into place the shapes you chose.

7. Decorate using glitter and paint. Keep in mind the traditional colors of red, white, gold, silver, and a little black for accent.

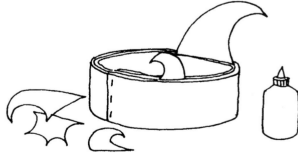

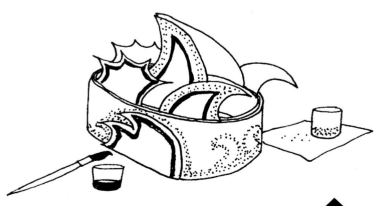

This **German Mardi Gras** is called Fasching or Karneval. It starts November 11 and ends in mid-March. The reveling leads to the Lenten period of fasting. Royalty and parades celebrate Fasching.

POISSON D'AVRIL

POISSON D'AVRIL

APRIL 1 IS FISH DAY IN FRANCE

Materials: salt dough ingredients, paper clip, dental floss or fish line, mobile devices (a hanger, branch or dowels), acrylic or tempera paint, brushes, bowl, cookie sheet.

1. Study pictures of the fish in your area. The fish in our photograph are Alaska salmon as they arrive at their spawning beds. The fish in your waters may look very different. You can also create fish using your imagination.

2. Follow the salt dough recipe mixing salt and flour in a bowl. Slowly add luke-warm water until a firm dough forms. Divide your dough into 6 or 7 equal parts.

3. Form the dough into a fish. Here is a pattern you may want to use.

4. Insert 2/3 of the paper clip end into the top of the dough formed fish.

5. Bake on a cookie sheet. Check the dough after 20 minutes.

6. Paint your fish or leave them natural. Tie your hanging thread through the paper clip end and then to the mobile form.

Salt Dough Recipe
(enough for 6-7 fish)

1/2	cup salt
1	cup all-purpose flour
1/4 - 1/2	cup water
2-4	drops of veg. oil

Mix and knead ingredients. Keep covered until use. Bake at 350 degrees for 20-25 minutes.

Trace around me

April 1 is a day when friends find ways to make fools out of each other. In France, April 1 is called **Poisson d'Avril** or "April Fish." Its origin may stem from a calendar change in 1564. New Year's Day was changed from April 1 to January 1. Because news traveled slowly people played tricks on those who celebrated the wrong New Year's Day. On this day in France the fish symbol is the theme for baked goods and candies.

UKRAINIAN PYSANKY EGGS

Ukrainian Pysanky Eggs

A Russian springtime tradition

Materials: one "blown" egg (see instructions on pages 2-3), wide and fine tip markers, glue, scissors, extra thin, brightly colored craft paper, glitter.

1. Color a blown egg all one light pastel color with marker. Hold egg gently in palm of hand as this is done. It helps to have a tissue covering your hand and remember to press *gently* on the egg to avoid cracking.

2. Collect several small scraps of craft paper. Choose a color scheme of 3 to 5 colors. Fold your paper in half and cut elaborate but very small shapes on the fold.

3. You may cut any shapes but try to think of symbols common to Easter and spring. (Think of symbols such as plants, flowers, and stars). Cut 2 or more of the same shape at the same time. For example:

4. Begin by gluing 1 of your shapes on the top or bottom end of the egg. This will give you a starting point. From here you can gently glue other shapes around this one creating a balanced or symmetrical design.

5. Shapes may be glued on top of one another.

6. Fine tip markers can be used by pressing gently to create details within the paper shapes or to outline the shapes.

7. Glue on a small amount of glitter for detail.

Pysanky eggs symbolize new beginnings such as a wedding, a new baby, a new home, graduation or a new job. They are also given in the spring— representing a new season of life.

FOLK ART FROM INDIA

Folk art from India is easy to identify. The colors are rich in reds, purples, and blues. Gold is popular and often mirrors are sewn into the pattern, almost as an eye looking at the world. The Hindu faith with its gods and goddesses dominate the carving, embroidery and painting of India.

Can you find the fabrics with the mirrors sewn onto them, the elephant on the temple toy

MAY

May is a month of fresh starts, romance, joy and welcome colors. Flowers, maypoles and new growth mark May as the holiday of the people, the workers. Today, May 1 has a military emphasis in some countries.

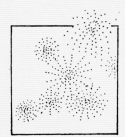

URINI NAL is Korea's Children's Day. It is celebrated May 5 and has been a tradition since 1919. Schools close on this day and carnivals offer children free rides. There are popular wrestling matches and tug-of-war contests in the park. Bakeries have free tastes for the children, theaters may open their doors at great discounts and in general Korean children have quite a holiday. The traditional drum song and dance is always performed with little girls invited to join the trained dancers just on this day.

MAY DAY has been an important first day for hundreds of years. Flowers have always been gathered. Trees have been used for poles and dancing in many forms has revolved around this "maypole". Queens of the May have been elected since Medieval times. Hawaii has "Lei Day" with contests awarding the most beautiful lei.

CINCO DE MAYO is Mexico's holiday honoring the successful battle at Puebla in 1862 when the Mexican army drove out the French army sent by Napoleon III. On this day the battle is reenacted by the Mexicans. The sounds of fiesta fill the air along with fireworks and mariachi music. This is one of the holidays when the pinata is enjoyed by the children.

MEMORIAL DAY, May 30, is the day to remember those who died while serving their country. This holiday has been extended to include all those who have died in the family. Families fly the American flag and visit graves to place flowers on them.

PISTA NG ANIHAN is the Philippine celebration of abundant harvest. It is held on May 15. Townspeople decorate their homes with hanging corn and coconuts and place fruit in windows and on doorways. Sometimes an owner will decorate his home according to his profession. Anoks or straw figures like scarecrows may be displayed. Among the highlights are the bird dance, the firecrackers and the parades of the water buffalo.

The **CHINESE DRAGON BOAT FESTIVAL** is a spring gala with competitions involving the racing of traditional finely carved boats with dragon heads and tails.

JUNE

June is the month traditionally marked for weddings. White blossoms for wedding bouquets are bridal wreath, orange blossom and gardenias all June bloomers.

June 23 is the **GREAT FEAST** in Mecca. This occasion commemorates the pilgrim's participating in the annual pilgrimage to Mecca as a part of the Islamic religious year.

June 13 is **ST. ANTHONY'S DAY**. He is the benefactor of children and animals. In Spain the people wear giant heads and stroll through the streets of Padua where St. Anthony was born.

FATHER'S DAY on the third Sunday in June was introduced in 1910 in Spokane, Washington. President Woodrow Wilson recognized the day in 1916 but it was not a national holiday until 1972. On this day children recognize their fathers or a special male figure and show their appreciation by doing things together.

During the month of June, Afro-Americans celebrate **JUNETEENTH**. On the nineteenth they celebrate their heritage with song, food, exhibits, and family gatherings.

JULY

July has a patriotic flavor. It just happens that July is a month of achieved independence. Space exploration has many impressive firsts that are commemorated in July.

On July 20, 1969, the first human landed on the moon. The landing was made from the spaceship Apollo II module Columbia. The astronauts were Michael Collins (who remained with the Columbia), Neil Armstrong and "Buzz" Aldrin. Armstrong and Aldrin walked on the moon for 2 hours and 15 minutes.

July 24 is **PIONEER DAY** in Utah. A parade features covered wagons and handcarts—reminders of the trek of the Mormon pioneers across the central American plains in 1847.

July 14 is France's Day of Independence and is called **BASTILLE DAY**. The Bastille was a state prison in Paris. On July 14, 1789, it was captured and partly destroyed in the French Revolution. Capturing the Bastille and releasing prisoners of the King and nobles encouraged the revolutionaries. Eventually the monarchy was overthrown. Today an open plaza marks the location of the prison and declares France's hard-won liberty.

July 1 is **DOMINION DAY** in Canada, a birthday celebration with parades and red and white maple-leaf flags. The first fruits of the harvest are celebrated worldwide.

On July 4th, 1776 America declared its independence from Britian with the signing of the Declaration of Independence in Philadelphia. On **INDEPENDENCE DAY** Americans light fireworks, enjoy friends and family gatherings, and hold patriotic flag-raising ceremonies. Red, white and blue are dominant colors. Independence day was first celebrated in 1777 when the Revolutionary War was still being fought.

AUGUST

August is the beginning of the harvest celebrations which may extend two and three months. Summer is on the wane. Throughout the world people are enjoying festivals honoring friendship and community.

Native Americans celebrate **HARVEST TIME**, cultural values and their renowned arts and crafts in events throughout America. The public is usually invited to witness traditional dancing, eat tribal foods and participate in auctions, games, and cultural commemorations.

August 1 was "**HONEY DAY**" in pre-revolutionary Russia and is enjoying a revival. A similar "first fruits" crop celebration occurs in Great Britain. Bread loaves are made from early harvested grains. In Ireland the first day is celebrated with berry picking and picnicking.

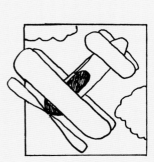

NATIONAL AVIATION DAY is August 19. This is the birthday of aviation pioneer Orville Wright, who made the first controlled flight in a power driven airplane. Though the flight took only 12 seconds, it is one of the most exciting events in aviation history.

RAMADAN in the Muslim world is a changing date determined by the moon. This important festival reminds the faithful of when the first revelations of the Koran were made known to Muhammad, the Holy Prophet. The Koran is the sacred book of the Islamic religion. Fasting, pure and kind thoughts, scripture reading and personal sacrifice are practices of devout Muslims.

MEXICAN CASCARONES

MEXICAN CASCARONES

A FESTIVE PARTY FAVOR FOR A MEXICAN CELEBRATION

Materials: 1 raw egg, colored paper 8 1/2" x 11", colored tissue paper, glue, stapler, scissors, colored paper scraps for confetti, tape.

1. Gently poke holes into the ends of your egg with the sharp end of a pair of scissors. One end can be the size of an adult finger nail. Hold the egg above a bowl and blow out the liquid inside. Lean your egg against a support and let it drain. *This must all be done gently or the egg will crack or break. See pages 2 and 3 for more detailed instructions.*

2. Measure a flat triangle 8" x 8" on your colored paper. Cut it out.

3. Prepare your colored tissue by cutting 2" folds that are staggered in length. Choose one of the designs here or create a new one:

4. Glue or staple the tissue paper by overlapping it on the flat triangle. Add tissue paper streamers at the narrow and wide ends.

5. Carefully bring the cone edges together and glue or staple.

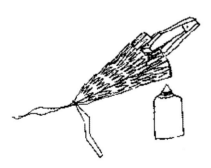

6. Cut tiny squares of confetti from the tissue scraps or colored paper. Scoop them into your *dried* blown egg. Seal the blow hole with tape. Glue your egg in the opening at the top of the cone. Have the sealed hole face into the cone so it cannot be seen.

7. At the point of celebration everyone bonks another person on their head with the cascarone until the egg breaks and sprays the confetti. Viva La Mexico!!

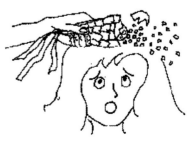

September 16 is **Mexican Independence Day** and is launched with the ringing of bells. Miguel Hidalgo's ringing of a bell and cry of "Viva la Independencia!" in 1810 launched Mexico's fight for independence. Fireworks, a national lottery, confetti and streamers mark the celebration.

CHI WARA HAT

CHI WARA HAT

FOR A MALI PLANTING FESTIVAL

Materials: black cardboard, an assortment of large and small shapes, scissors, glue, stapler, tempera paint, raffia or dried grasses, tape.

1. Measure a strip of cardboard 6" thick and long enough to go around the upper part of your head like a crown. Staple or glue it together. It should be at least 6" wide and usually 24" long.

2. Attach a piece of cardboard across the top in one of the ways suggested. Glue. Let dry.

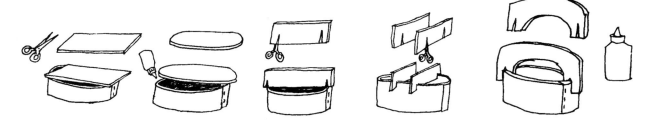

3. With smaller scraps of cardboard add a variety of forms typical of the Chi Wara to your hat. Build it as high as you can. Below are some ideas from hats in museums.

4. Punch holes and add raffia or dried grasses to the base, the back and along the sides. Tape them down on the inside of your hat.

Chi Wara hats are worn by the Mambara people in the African country of Mali. The symbol represents an antelope—important for its swiftness as game and for its actions which are copied in dance form at the **Chi Wara Festival**. This festival is about planting and honors seeds, sowing, rain and all things that produce an abundant crop. All of Africa celebrates planting festivals essential to food production.

FATHER'S DAY PRINTS

FATHER'S DAY PRINTS

PAPER TIES AND WRAPPING PAPER FROM VEGETABLE PRINTS

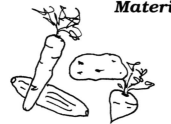

Materials: hard vegetables (such as potatoes, carrots, or turnips), small safe knife, sharp pencil, acrylic or tempera paint, sponge, rag or cheap brush, any lightweight paper at least 15" wide and any length, tray for paint, water.

1. Think about the person you are doing this project for. What images can you imagine that are about a hobby, work, favorite food, sport, etc.? Draw the image in its simplest form on a piece of paper.

2. If it is a big image choose a brown baker potato. Cut it in half lengthwise and draw the form on the top. Cut around the image on the top of the potato. Cut deeply down the sides. Your image should be raised 1/4" above the rest of the potato. Dry the juicy surface of your potato.

3. Pour your paint for printing onto a paper plate or a foil covered surface. Brush, sponge or dab the paint on your dried veggie surface. Experiment by printing on scrap paper.

4. Lay out your 15" tie paper. Cut your tie pattern from a folded piece of newspaper or a real tie. Trace around it on the newspaper. Do not cut it out until after you have printed it. Lay out your paper for gift wrapping as well. Print your tie and paper. Cut out the tie after the paint has dried. Use the rest for wrapping paper.

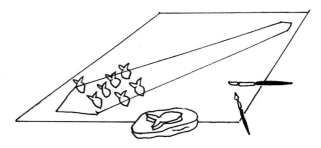

Other printing ideas:

1. With a clean eraser and washable marker draw a simple form on the eraser and print. After each print, mark the eraser again and continue printing.

2. Glue a felt shape onto a wooden block. Brush with paint and print.

JAPANESE CARP KITE

JAPANESE CARP KITE

A CELEBRATION OF CHILDREN'S DAY

Materials: 24" x 36" piece of butcher paper (any color), tissue paper scraps, 1" x 24" cardboard strip or 24" piece of wire, glue, scissors, stapler, markers, crepe paper or ribbon for streamers, hole punch, 3 1-foot lengths of string, long pole (optional).

1. First fold over 1" of the short side of your tissue paper. Place your 24" strip of wire, or cardboard in the fold and glue.

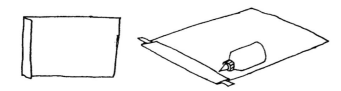

2. Next fold your tissue paper in half the long way. Glue it along the edge with a small amount of glue. Let dry.

3. Insert a folded newspaper between the tissue sheets to protect the underside. With the markers draw and color in the shape of a large fish. The mouth will be near the end with the fold.

4. Glue on tissue paper fish scales, fins, eyes, gills, etc. from the tissue scraps. Add long streamers on the tail if you wish.

5. Bend the wire or cardboard to form an open circle at the mouth end of your kite. Staple the cardboard to strengthen the circle.

6. Tie on the 3 strings to the "mouth" of your kite and attach to a long pole. Hang outside on a bright sunny day.

On May 5, Japan celebrates **Tango-no-seku**, traditionally Boy's Day but now adopted as Children's Day: Kodomo-no-hi. Carp banners are flown from rooftops with each fish representing the number of sons in the family. It is common for boys to do a display of warrior implements and dolls. A special bean cake is eaten and parents give thanks for their healthy sons. The carp is a symbol of courage, power and determination, as it swims against the current. Small boys crawl through the paper carp kites from mouth to tail. If the paper is not torn or punctured the child will have good luck.

FOLK ART FROM AFRICA

African folk art is entwined with the seasons, harvest and rites of passage such as reaching adolescence. Folk art is purposeful and meant to be combined with dance and feasts. Often the two honor an animal represented in the costumes. The feast is to enjoy a bountiful yield or change in season. The natural world dominates crafts, and these are typical of the variety found in Africa past and present.

Can you find the blue, beaded, face mask, the heavy round, amber trade bead necklac

he elephants painted on the cup, the tube-like dart holder and the fancy silver

HAT & STREAMER STICK

4TH OF JULY HAT & STREAMER STICK

Materials: 18" x 24" sheet of blue railroad board, red and white construction paper, red, white and blue tissue paper, 1 stick (a chopstick works well), glue, stapler, scissors, gold star stickers.

The Uncle Sam Hat

1. Cut railroad board into an 8" x 18" strip to fit around your head. Cut red and white paper into 1" x 8" strips. Make 6 red and 6 white strips. Glue onto blue railroad board leaving 1" for blue space. Repeat the red, white and blue pattern. You may glue gold stars on the white strips or make an eraser stamp with a yellow marker and stamp them on. See page 41 for instructions.

2. Shape into cylinder to fit on your head. Staple the end into place. Place cylinder on a piece of railroad board and trace around the cylinder. Repeat this step again and cut one for the top of the hat. On the other draw a larger circle around the cylinder. Draw three 2" tabs on the inside of the inner circle. Cut out the inner circle but leave the tabs. Fold the tabs up. Place the hat on the railroad board with the tabs inside. Glue them to the hat. Let dry. Trim off the extra to make the brim.

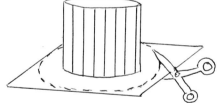

Streamer Stick

In this project you are combining tissue paper and construction paper strips. One is feather-light and one will hold stars.

1. Cut red, white, and blue tissue paper into 1/2" strips of varying lengths.
   Cut 10 of each color.
   Cut 6 1/2" strips of blue construction paper 10 " long.
   Cut a 1" strip of blue construction paper 6" long.
   Cut 6 stars from white or yellow construction paper or use gold stars.

2. Gather all cut tissue paper and blue construction paper strips together. Lay them on the tip of the stick. Wrap the 1" x 6" strip of blue paper around them tightly and glue it down. Hold and let it dry. Curl the blue construction paper strips by wrapping them around a pencil. Glue stars on the ends of the blue paper.

Americans celebrate the signing of the **Declaration of Independence** on July 4, 1776 in the United States with picnics, parades and fireworks.

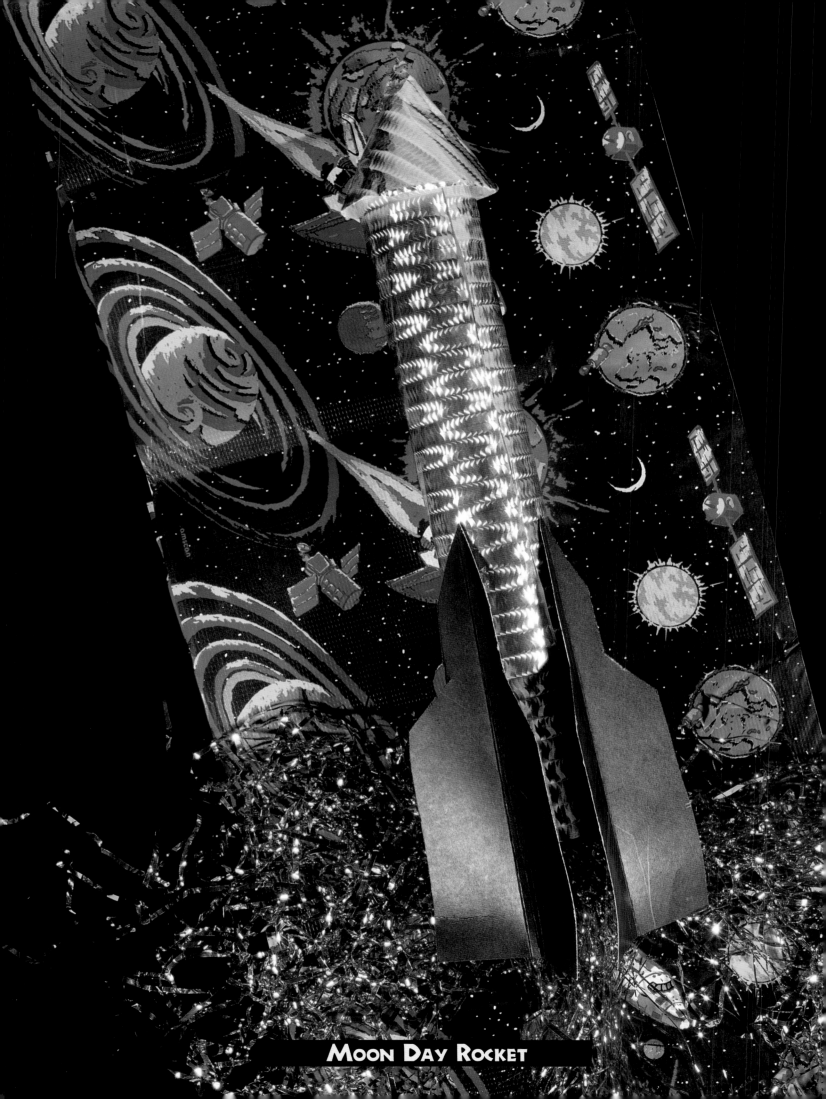

MOON DAY ROCKET

Moon Day Rocket

CELEBRATE THE FIRST MOON WALK WITH A ROCKET PROJECT

Materials: a wide cardboard tube between 12" and 15" inches long, red, yellow, and orange tissue, foil or shiny silver wrapping paper, black cardboard 12" x 20", scissors, glue, stapler, pencil, ruler.

1. Look at pictures of rockets.

2. Lay out silver paper on the wrong side. Cut it to cover your tube.

3. Find something that is an 8" circle. Trace around it on the wrong side of the silver paper. Cut out the circle.

4. Cut out a wedge and fold into a cone (A). Size it to your rocket tube (B). Staple the circle into a cone when it is the right size (C). Now glue or tape it to the rocket tube (D).

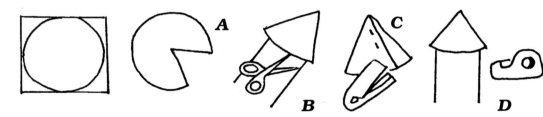

5. Cut narrow strips of tissue paper and foil. Staple them together in bunches, and glue them inside the rocket tube.

6. Cut 3 rocket buttress supports from the black cardboard. Score a middle line and fold each in half. Glue the folded cardboard spine back to the rocket outside, extending the buttress wings beyond the rocket base 2" so the rocket is "lifted" off of the ground.

Moon Day was established on July 20, 1969, when the first humans walked on the moon. U.S. astronauts Neil Armstrong and Edwin Arlin, Jr. were the first to take the historic walk. They brought back rocks, moon matter and photographs. Neil Armstrong hit a golf ball with a makeshift golf club.

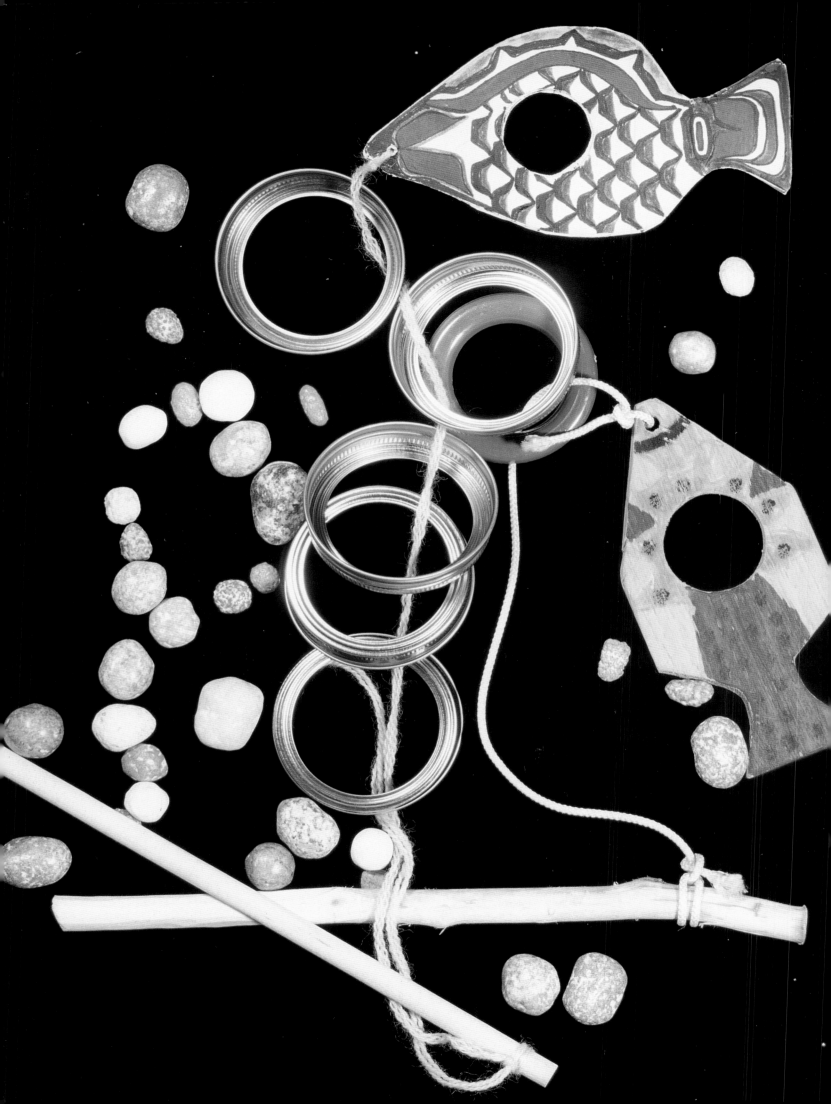

POMBAWONGA

A NATIVE AMERICAN RING AND PIN GAME

Materials: 4 pieces of cardboard 6" x 6", at least 16" of strong string, eight 3" diameter rings (metal canning rings work well or plastic rings), a 14" stick, strong twig or dowel, glue, scissors, markers, crayons or oil pastels.

1. Make the fish by cutting 4 identical cardboard shapes with a 1 1/4" hole cut out of their centers. Glue 2 flat shapes together and put a weight on them while they dry. Using 2 layers makes the fish stronger and heavier.

2. Decorate both sides of the paper fish with Native American designs (one of our fish has Northwest Coast Indian designs). You could also decorate the fish with creative patterns. Use markers, crayons or oil pastels.

3. Attach the string securely at one end of the stick and the other end through the fish's mouth.

4. Hold the string upside down and loop the rings from the stick end through until they hit the fish. Now you are ready to play Pombawonga.

How to play the game: The object of the game is simply to catch all the rings on the end of the stick, one at a time, and finally to catch the fish through its hole in the center. The stick must be held opposite the string-tied end.

August and September feature **Native American** celebrations of harvest and unity. A game such as this might be crafted and played. Ring and pin games of skill are played under a variety of names in many parts of the world. The Eskimos call the game *ajaqaq*, the English *bilbocatch* and the French *bilboquet*.

Chusongnal

CHUSONGNAL

A KOREAN HAT TRADITIONALLY WORN AT HARVEST TIME

Materials: construction paper 14" x 28" (1 per person, any color but usually white), scissors, stapler, tissue paper squares from approximately 5" to 10", colored paper scraps, markers, found fabric scraps (such as trim, rickrack, ribbon and lace), glue.

1. Fold the large sheet of 14" x 28" construction paper in half bringing the short edges together.

2. Next fold the 2 short edges back about 2" as shown.

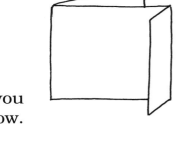

3. Open the paper and fold the bottom edge as shown.

4. Keeping the paper in the same position, work it so you fold it so it resembles the dotted line in the picture below. This may take a few tries.

5. Staple the top edge together.

6. Make large tissue paper flowers and glue and staple them to the hat. Decorate the folded edges with markers, paper or fabric trim.

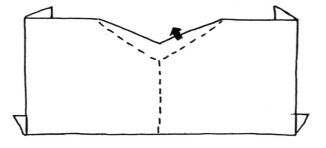

7. Staple or tape on 2 strings for ties.
Attach them to the center of the inside of each side of your hat.

Chusongnal is the Korean day for Thanksgiving. The word means "autumn night" and is especially meaningful to farmers. They parade through the streets with ribboned hats that create streamers of color as they dance and sway with the music, playing the traditional Korean drum and carrying a farm tool. This is also a day for remembering ancestors by offering five special foods: dates, apples, chestnuts, pears and persimmons. Girls perform the "Circle Dance" which symbolically asks the moon for good luck.

Can you find the sun, moon, Adam and Eve, figures on the tree of life, the little clay bu[...]

FOLK ART FROM MEXICO

Folk art from Mexico is a specialty of certain regions. Suns, animals, flourishing plant life, fish and birds may glow from a lacquered box or a woven rug. Ancient figures have been adapted to a Christian faith in clay, embroidery and basketry. The tree of life may be standing in a shrine or in a niche in a home.

the lacquered chicken, the hat with the ribbons and pompoms? *Answers on page 81.*

September

September is a time of harvest. Cornhusk wreaths, straw dollies and animals are made to encourage an abundant yield. In the Orient rice is colored. In Africa yams and peanuts are celebrated, and the Native American honors corn. Most states hold a state fair as a way of awarding excellence in produce, stock and handcrafts. September is also a back-to-school month. Children of all ages prepare for that important first day.

Germany also celebrates **OKTOBERFEST** (except it comes in September). The King of Bavaria celebrated the first folk festival in 1810 to honor his son's marriage. Since then Germans throughout the world have danced, played folk tunes and enjoyed German foods for the duration of the sixteen-day festival. If you were to have an **OKTOBERFEST** you would wear a dirndl dress or lederhosen (leather pants). You would eat apple strudel and bratwurst and dance the polka to accordion music. Munich is the German city most famous for this event.

STATE FAIRS are held throughout America as a form of a "harvesting" celebration. Cash prizes and ribbons are awarded to the winning produce, finest animals, highest quality handcrafted items, best recipes, and other elements of "bringing in the bounty." Usually entertainment, a carnival, demonstrations and local specialties are anticipated elements of the fair.

POTLATCHES are celebrations given traditionally by the Pacific Northwest Indians. These elaborate feasts feature dancing, theatricals, story-songs about heroes, historical events and the acquisition of objects. Gifts used to be given to the guests. Potlatches are not just "parties." They are held by a clan for a specific reason and usually there is a purpose stated in the invitations.

The Navajo Indians gather the second week of September in Window Rock, Arizona for the **NAVAJO INDIAN FAIR**. This event is to honor the old ways of life and features native food, rodeo events, a beauty contest and ancient songs and music.

October

October is "discovery" month as American shores attracted foreign explorers. October is also the end of a season of plenty and harvest and the eve of a season of cold, darkness and foreboding. Light, costumes and masks, treats and symbols of fright have appeared for centuries in October.

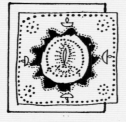

DIWALI is India's Festival of Lights, one of the most beautiful events in the country. Women decorate their floors with alpanas, elaborate designs in paint or rice powder. Children make dipas, tiny clay saucers with wicks, and line all ledges, rooftops, and paths with the little lights.

Two days in October celebrate the discovery of America. October 9 is celebrated as **LEIF ERICSON DAY** by Norwegian-Americans. Eric the Red was the father of Leif Ericson who discovered Greenland and then sailed further west to find still another new land. Scientists have found Viking artifacts and the remains of the Newfoundland Viking Village.

COLUMBUS DAY is October 12 and is celebrated in America as well as in Spain. Christopher Columbus was Italian but the King and Queen of Spain gave him the support to explore. Still, Italy is proud and shares the honor along with many South and Central American countries.

Europeans and Americans celebrate a modern day vestige of an ancient tradition to scare away all evil spirits the eve before winter was thought to begin. It was called "All Hallows' Eve" and was shortened to **HALLOWEEN**. Today it is a night when children dress in masks and costumes and go from door to door threatening a trick if they do not get a treat. School carnivals have become a popular neighborhood approach to celebrating this event.

56

NOVEMBER

This early winter/late autumn month features elections in the USA. November 11 commemorates the end of World War I in 1918. It is called Veterans' Day, Remembrance Day and Armistice Day....observed in many different countries.

THANKSGIVING is one of America's most popular holidays. Celebrated on the fourth Thursday of November, it is marked by family gatherings and the traditional turkey dinner. Hardships of the early Pilgrims and the benevolence of the Native Americans prompted the first Thanksgiving feast in America. It was proclaimed a holiday in 1789.

Children in England call out "A penny for the GUY" as they carry a straw-filled dummy through the streets receiving coins. It is **GUY FAWKES DAY**, November 5, and most towns or neighborhoods have spent many days adding fuel to a mammoth community bonfire. Guy Fawkes was caught attempting to blow up King James I in 1605. He was one of the many who felt the king was unfair to Roman Catholics. When the bonfire is lit all the straw figures are thrown onto the top.

Children hold lantern parades throughout Germany with carved turnips holding candles. Originally they were held on **ST. MARTIN'S DAY**, November 11. St. Martin was a saint who died around 400 A.D. Also associated with this day is eating a goose. Protestants celebrate the day as well, because Martin Luther was born on November 10.

African agricultural people celebrate the **HARVEST** of their major crops (yams, peanuts and corn depending on the area of Africa) with dancing, feasts and masks. The scene of a tribal harvest is rich in sounds and sights and the smells of roasting yams, peanut soup, corn and other rewards of summer's hard work.

LOY KRATHONG is Thailand's autumn festival about the honoring of water. Forgiveness is asked if water has been polluted and leaf boats are floated down the river Nammanda symbolizing the "footprints" of Buddha. Thai children decorate banana leaf boats with flowers. They fill their leaf "cup" with incense, a candle, a coin and then launch the tiny vessel down the river. According to legend, if a child's candlelight lasts until the boat disappears a wish will come true. People line the river banks to watch and enjoy the moving sea of tiny lights and the fireworks exploding overhead.

Feasts: Every country celebrates the family gathering and an abundance of special foods.
• In Sweden the feast is a buffet called a "Smorgasbord" and features marinated fish.
• In Poland and Lithuania families share a good luck wafer.
• Serbians cover their dining table with straw as a symbol of the stable in the Nativity scene.
• Czechoslovakians leave one seat empty for the Christ Child.
• Danes hang a sheaf of wheat from a pole for the birds.
• In England the plum pudding may hold four things: a ring indicating the first person to marry, the thimble predicting an old maid, a button meant to confirm bachelorhood and a coin promising riches.

December features the evergreen tree, symbol of Winter Soltice. Celebrations include Kwanzaa, the African harvest event; Christmas, the Christian remembrance of the birth of Christ; and Hanukkah, an eight-day Jewish celebration.

DECEMBER

Light: The decorated evergreen tree springs from the Druid Oak story. It is said that Martin Luther brought the first tree inside and added candles. Each country decorates the tree differently. In Poland people attach feathers, ribbons and colored paper. Lithuanians make little bird cages and windmills for decorations. Scandinavians hang straw ornaments. Germans use delicate glass baubles. Some form of light is usually given to the tree and a star for the top is traditional.

SANTA LUCIA ushers in the Christmas season in Sweden with a breakfast tray of "cat buns" and hot chocolate. Santa Lucia wears an evergreen crown with seven candles aglow on her head.

HANUKKAH, the "feast of lights," begins on the 25th day of the Hebrew month and lasts for eight days, with the family lighting a new candle on the menorah each night.

SCHULTUTE

SCHULTÜTE

A GERMAN SCHOOL GIFT

Materials: White or pale-colored sturdy paper 18" x 22" (the larger the cone the better), ruler, markers, crayons, scrap paper, scissors, glue, decorative things such as ribbon, glitter, fabric trim, braid, tape, hole punch, stapler, string.

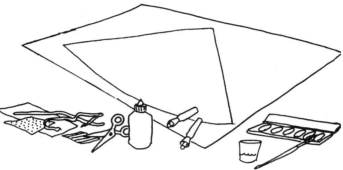

1. To make your own Schultute you will first need to make a large cone out of the 18" x 22" construction paper. Make a triangle that measures longer across the top than the sides.

2. Cut it out.

3. While your triangle is laying flat, decorate it with crayons, markers and watercolors. You may use realistic scenes or designs. Use the watercolors to color what you created. When dry, glue on any found objects you wish.

4. To roll the triangle into a cone, place your finger at the bottom point and roll the sides. Have a friend help you. Staple or tape the side.

5. Cut and trim the uneven edges at the large opening. Add a strong handle after punching 2 holes. Fill it with school supplies and goodies.

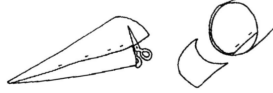

School children in Germany are given a large paper cone filled with candy and school supplies for their first day of school. The goody-filled cone is called a **Schulute** (shool tootuh). It symbolizes the wish that the student will have a rich education in the years ahead.

Perhaps a class could make and decorate some cones and fill them with surprises and present them to a kindergarten class in your school. Share the German meaning of the craft with them as well.

AFRICAN MASK

African Mask

A TRADITIONAL HARVEST MASK

Materials: construction paper (18" x 24" 1 per person), paper scraps, scissors, glue, raffia or dried grasses, hole punch, pencil, dried grains and beans.

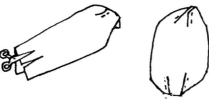

1. Cut 2 to 3 slits 3-4" deep into the top edge of the 18" x 24" construction paper. Fold these over one another and staple into place. This forms the top of your mask and will rest on the top of your head.

2. Cut slits into the bottom edge and repeat as in step 1, or simply cut the bottom edge into an interesting shape.

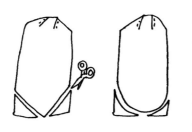

3. Hold your mask up to your face and have a partner help you locate where the eyeholes will be. Mark location. Cut them out.

4. Punch holes on either side for the string that will hold your mask on. (Make the holes above your ears).

5. Decorate your mask by gluing on paper scraps. Fold, bend, roll or score the paper to create more three-dimensional forms.

6. Glue on the found objects.

fold   bend   roll   score

Harvest season bursts with celebrations in western Africa. Tribes live very close to nature and depend on the right amount of rain and sun for successful crops. A good harvest is an occasion for special thanksgiving.

The **Ashanti** show their thanks by sacrificing a sheep at their yam harvest. The ripe yams and fat sheep are meant to please the gods who have helped the crop succeed.

The **Yoruba** combine the yam festival with a ceremony to honor the ancestors. A few members of the tribe are chosen to be the "spirit dancers" representing the spirits of the dead in long robes and masks.

The **Ga** tribe has a harvest called "hunger hooting". Like the Yoruba and Ashanti they offer the gods their harvest, but their offering is corn.

BALERO

BALERO

A POPULAR GAME FROM MEXICO

Materials: any sturdy paper for the cone that is 11" x 14", markers or crayons, scissors, glue, stapler, hole punch, a wooden bead or heavy button for the ball, 24" of string.

1. Lay your posterboard flat and measure a cone 11 " along the side and 14 " across the top.

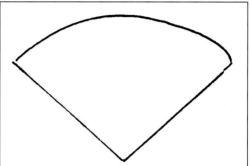

2. Before you cut it out, decorate your paper with patterns from Mexico using markers or crayons. Here are some good examples.

3. Staple the sides of the cone and glue the bottom tip .

4. Punch 1 hole near the top edge of the cone.

5. A) Cut string about 2 feet long. B) Put one end through the hole you have made with a hole punch and knot the string on the inside. C) Tie your ball to the other end of the string.

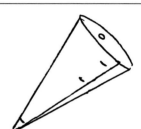

A version of a game such as **balero** is played throughout the world. In Mexico you might see competing players vie for a prize. All ages enjoy **balero**. Fiestas occur throughout the year in Mexico. Some other common features of the events are masks, fireworks, paper carts and pinatas.

DAY OF THE DEAD

DAY OF THE DEAD

A SKELETON MARIONETTE

Materials: 2 pieces of cardboard 4" x 8", scissors, glue, brads, hole punch, string, flat sticks, masking tape, tempera paint, small brushes and a pencil.

1. On 1 of the 4" x 8" pieces of cardboard draw the head, neck and body of your marionette. Cut it out.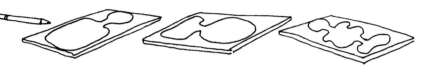

2. On the other piece of 4" x 8" cardboard draw 2 leg and 2 arm forms. Make certain they are at least 1/2" to 1" wide. They may be any shape. Cut out the arms and legs.

3. With a hole punch make a hole at both shoulders and upper arms and attach with a brad. Do the same with the legs. (You may also cut both arms and legs in half, punching holes and attaching brads to create knees and elbows).

4. Paint your skeleton all white. Let dry.

5. Attach a flat stick to the back with glue and masking tape.

6. Cut 4 strings 12" long. Staple the end of each to the top of each arm and leg above the brad. Tie all 4 strings together at the bottom.

Mexico celebrates the **Day of the Dead** on November 2. It is a celebration about honoring the spirits of deceased ances- tors. On this day the Mexican tree of life candleholder is taken to the cemetery where the candles are lit and it adorns the family grave. The tree of life is decorated with birds, angels and flowers to symbolize heavenly messengers. Along with the candles, food is left for the deceased. The spirit of the dead are invited to join the family and share in the feast. It has been traditionally believed that this friendly gesture will appease them and keep them friendly so they will cause the family to prosper and have good luck. At the home a shrine is made supporting the photographs of the deceased and flanked by marigolds. Skeletons appear as tie pins and puppets, and are sold as molds for candy. See the tree of life on pages 54 and 55.

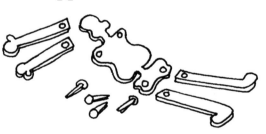

A Mummy and King Tut

A MUMMY AND KING TUT

A SARCOPHAGUS COVERED WITH HIEROGLYPHICS

Materials: a small, long balloon, file folder cardboard, glue, tape, scissors, pencil, newspaper, wide and fine-tip markers of many colors, tempera paint, a serrated knife, flour, water, sandpaper.

1. Blow up your balloon and knot the end. Lay it in the middle of the flat cardboard. Measure it and mark the cardboard, scoring lines around the balloon. Then cut and fold the sides around the balloon. Tape the edges.

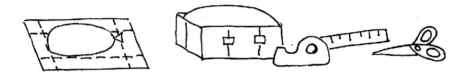

2. Now you are going to papier mache around the box and the balloon. Cut newspaper strips 1" to 2" wide and 6" to 8" long. Cut about 25 for each box. Make a flour paste by mixing 1 cup of flour with 1/2 cup warm water. Mix until smooth. (Protect your working surface with paper).

3. Dip each paper strip into the flour paste. Pull the wet strip between 2 fingers to strip off extra paste. Layer each wet strip over the balloon box. Everything must be covered with paper strips when you are finished. Smooth the edges as best you can.

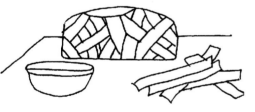

4. Let your box dry overnight. Prop it up so air can circulate around it. It is dry when it is hard to the touch and of a white color. Sand surface to smooth the uneven edges. Adult supervision is recommended.

5. Cut the top off carefully with a serrated knife. Puncture and remove the balloon.

6. Paint your box with white tempera paint. Let it dry. Now decorate with pencil hieroglyphics and symbols of ancient Egypt.

November 26, 1922, is the date Howard Carter, a British archeologist entered **King Tutankhamen's** tomb. This discovery allowed us to learn about ancient Egyptian culture. Though this is not a calendar celebration it is an event of importance in the study of other cultures.

Can you find the thousand folded origami cranes, the teapot with a traditional symbol for

FOLK ART FROM JAPAN

Japanese art is one of the world's great cultural legacies. Bonsai plant designs, Ikebana, the art of arranging flowers, even packaging is an art form with the Japanese. Craftspeople and artists have important stature in Japanese culture. Many western arists like Toulouse-Lautrec, Van Gogh and Gaugin were heavily influenced by Japanese art. Lacquer, porcelain, glazes and carved ivory show the skill of the Japanese artist.

happiness, the girl doll, the boy doll, the stone ball, the umbrella, the red kite?

Kwanzaa Day Candelabra

KWANZAA DAY
CELEBRATION CANDELABRA

AN AFRICAN HARVEST HOLIDAY

Materials: 3 green candles, 3 red candles, 1 black candle, a package of self-hardening clay.

1. A) Divide the clay into 2 large pieces and set one of them aside. B) Divide the other into 2 even pieces.

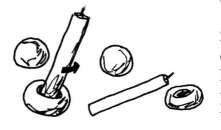

2. From the 2 pieces you just divided in step 1B, mold 1 of the pieces into seven balls. Turn them into candle holders by inserting the candle in the top of the ball and pressing. Rotate the candle to make sure the fit is not too tight to remove the candle. Repeat for the other balls of clay.

3. Mold the other piece of 1B into a base for the candelabra. Mold the large piece, 1A, into a foundation for the candle holders.

4. Attach the candleholders and base to the foundation and mold them together also. Scratching the surface of the clay, called scoring, helps the pieces stick together. Allow to dry overnight.

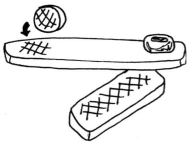

5. Place the colored candles as you see in the photo.

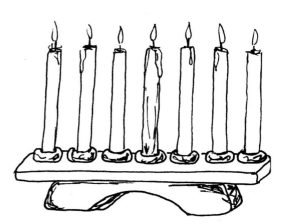

This popular new American holiday was first celebrated in 1966 as a celebration of the cultural roots of Afro-Americans. The holiday lasts from December 26 to January 1. **"Kwanzaa"** means "first fruits" in Swahili and many of the table decorations are foods of the harvest.

The traditional candelabrum is called a "kinara". Each candle color is important: black represents the color of the people, red their continuing struggle, and green the color of Mother Africa.

DOVES OF PEACE

DOVES OF PEACE

A PAPER ORNAMENT FOR THE SEASON OF PEACE

Materials: pencil, scissors, hole punch, glue, cardboard, thread, ribbon, dental floss or fish line.

Cut out as many "basic bird" shapes as you wish.
We have 3 variations:

Curly Bird:

Glue 2 birds together except at the tails. When the glue has dried cut the tails into 4 strips as shown. Wind each strip around a pen, pencil or knitting needle away from the other bird tail feathers.

To make curly bird wings cut a piece that is wing shaped. The dotted line on our patterns show where you slip the wing through. Fold the one-piece wing up to keep it from falling out. Now cut end strips and repeat the rolled curling process. Give your bird 2 eyes and thread the hanging material where it best balances.

Flutter Wing Bird:

Cut a slit along dots of the pattern. Cut out a wing pattern and slip it through the slit. Fold it up. Mark 2 eyes for your bird and string it for hanging where it balances best.

Flying Bird:

Take your bird, cut out and glue 2 wings to the back. Mark the eyes and string it for hanging where it balances best.

Flying Bird

Use these patterns to create your bird.

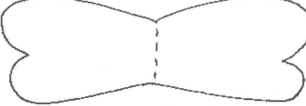

Flutter Wing Bird

SCANDINAVIAN NISSE

SCANDINAVIAN NISSE

A CHILDREN'S CHRISTMAS FIGURE

Materials: ruler, scissors, glue, pencil, red paper, white paper, beard material such as cotton, polyfill or wool fleece, fake or real fur, red and black fine-tip markers.

1. Trace the pattern on this page and cut out the figure. You may wish to adapt it in size. Measure the pattern widths and length. Cut your red paper long enough to fit about four patterns. Mark and measure four rectangles. Score each section for easy folding. Fold the paper accordion style.

2. Place your pattern and fit it on top of the accordion. Outline it with a pencil. *Be sure the edges touch the fold line.*

3. Cut out shape with scissors.

4. Draw a "face" pattern on white paper, cut 4 white pieces of paper. Reverse the pattern and cut 4 more.

5. Glue the face on both sides of the figure so it can be viewed front and back. Glue the beard below the face. Detail the face with eyes, nose, and red-dot cheeks.

Scandinavian countries have elfin figures bring presents to the children. In Finland there is the **Tomtuu**, in Norway the **Julnisse**, in Sweden the **Tomte** and in Denmark the **Nisse**. This gnome-like form is a symbol of good luck and prosperity providing he has been fed well with rice porridge on Christmas Eve.

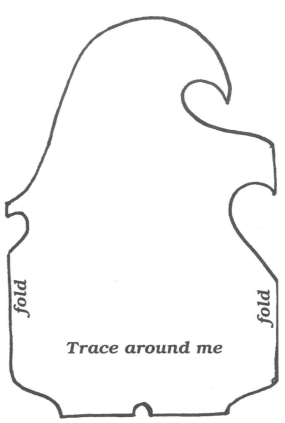

fold

fold

Trace around me

Donna Matthews originated this design.

INDEX

ACKNOWLEDGMENTS

Grateful appreciation to Barbara Baugh, whose support, encouragement and contributions made this project a reality.

The author and the Anchorage Museum of History and Art initiated some of the projects in this publication as part of a CELEBRATION exhibition for young people. This is the first opportunity to refine and publish the research and design that developed from this effort. Executive Director, Patricia B. Wolf, and Sharon Abbott, Curator of Education, generously shared the material.

Donna Matthews, a friend and business partner, initially created these projects and gave permission for their inclusion in this publication:
Woven Heart Basket
Doves of Peace
Scandinavian Nisse.

Donna Mack of the Anchorage store One People shared her folk art collection for photographs. Also, Donna freely gave her knowledge of indigenous people, their crafts and traditions. Her contributions and enthusiasm for the concept are appreciated.

Melinda Tietjen designed and made several of the crafts.

Jocelyn Young has read and re-read the text in most of its rough to finished stages. Her suggestions are of great value.

Kathy Veltre's friendship and caring influenced the book's quality.

Madlyn Tanner edited the early text. Su Richards assisted with information specifics.

Anchorage School District librarians Molly Bynum, Wendy Nyberg and Lynn Hallquist's knowledge and expertise about celebration topics and children's book publications influenced the book's content.

Reference Books on Celebrations

Cordello, Becky Stevens. *Celebrations*. New York: Butterick Publishing, 1977.
Lee, Nancy and Oldham, Linda. *Hands on Heritage, An Experiential Approach to Multicultural Education*. Long Beach, California: Hands on Publications, 1978.
Los Angeles County Museum of Art. *MEXICO: Splendors of Thirty Centuries*. Education Department: Los Angeles, 1976.
Mayhew, Martin and Cherille. *Fun with Art*. Cheadle, Cheshire: James & Galt Co. Ltd., 1970.
Parth, Linda and Chase, Josephine. *Multicultural Spoken Here: Discovering America's People Through Language Arts and Library Skills*. Santa Monica, California: Goodyear Publishing Co. Inc., 1979.
Sarnoff, Jane and Ruffins, Reynold. *Light the Candles! Beat the Drums! A Book of Holidays*. New York: Charles Scribner's Sons, 1979.
Seattle Children's Museum. *Uwajimaya, Meeting Ground: Chinese Children, Chinese Friends*. Seattle: 1983.
Sayer, Chloe. *Crafts of Mexico*. Garden City, New York: Doubleday and Company Inc., 1977.
Thomassen-Grant, Inc. *Celebrations*. 1989 Travel Engagement Calendar. Charlottesville, Virginia: 1989.
UNICEF (United Nations Children's Fund). *Festivals and Celebrations Engagement Calendar*, 1981.

FOLK ART OF CENTRAL AND SOUTH AMERICA (Inside covers)

1. Jaguar head mask
2. Circle of figures that is a clay whistle. Whistles are an ancient music form in this region.
3. Snake patterned clay mask
4. Flute, believed to have originated in South America
5. The silver work which reflects the Spanish skill with metal
6. Embroidery and brocade on clothing reflecting a specific pattern and color of a region
7. Huichol beaded figures made to be left in holy places
8. Woven red Bolivian shawl
9. Woven piece from Ecuador
10. Mexican woven piece
11. Carved jaguar
12. Huichol cross-stiched bag
13. Transformation mask of a fish
14. Straw ball necklace from Ecuador
15. Leather braided sandal
16. Mola from the Cuna Indians

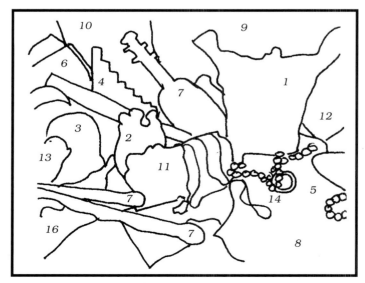

FOLK ART OF INDIA (page 32 and 33)

1. This gate canopy of mirrored and embroidered fabric is displayed on special occasions such as weddings, births, and annual festivals
2. A wooden box with a painted Hindu story
3. An embroidered fleece coat
4. Embroidered slippers worn by royalty
5. Elephant temple toy
6. Wagon temple toy
7. Wood horn with metal trim
8. A carved bath tool with a carved bird handle
9. Embroidered, woven and mirrored fabrics

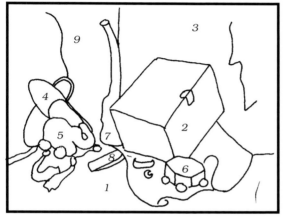

FOLK ART OF RUSSIA (page 18 and 19)

1. Nanai Birch Bark basket woven and embossed
2. Copper samovar
3. Gzhel plate with cobalt finish
4. Handcarved birch bark box from Pereslavl-Zeleskii, a village near Moscow
5. Nanai birch bark carved basket
6. Stainless steel samovar
7. Gzhel tea cup with gold and cobalt finish
8. Patterned wool scarf from Ivanovo
9. Old religious hymnal dated 1747
10. Enamel and silver spoon
11. Modern Russian rubles
12. Painted egg with the levkos technique
13. Gzhel sugar box
14. Pysanky egg from Rudenko
15. Filligree decorated egg
16. Birch bark powder box
17. Matrioshka (nesting) dolls
18. Rooster from Viatka
19. Tea cozy doll by Anna Kouzminikh, a fiber artist
20. Religious Matrioshka doll

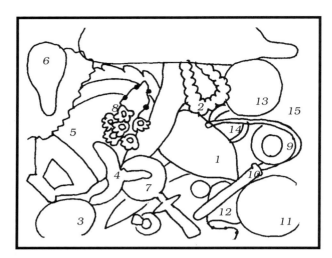

FOLK ART FROM AFRICA (page 44 and 45)

1. Carved, beaded face mask
2. African amber and trade beads from the 17th century
3. Kente cloth hat
4. Wedding necklace
5. Chi Wara carved wooden hat
6. Ancestral carved mask with raffia trim
7. Carved good luck charm of an infant carried by a pregnant woman
8. Necklace made from cooking pots

9. Circles from a palm leaf used as a pot support
10. Dart holder
11. Carved gourd cup etched with elephants
12. Beaded loin cloths: the light one is a woman's and the dark one is a man's
13. Design on the bottom of a woven basket
14. Courtship necklace
15. Mud cloth

FOLK ART FROM BALI (page 4 and 5)

1. A guardian figure, the winged angel might be depicted as a female form, a friendly monster or even a dragon. Traditionally the protective figure flies over the cradle.
2. The familiar carved wooden stick puppet
3. A colorful wood shavings tree form is typical of this craft
4. A carved feather plume of a fantastic bird
5. Pierced leather stick puppet
6. Batik fabrics
7. Painted cats, popular folk art of today

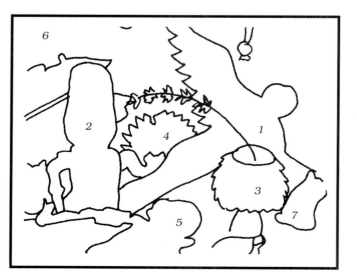

FOLK ART FROM JAPAN (page 68 and 69)

1. A beautifully crafted doll for display, not for play
2. A commonly used fabric divider of indigo blue called a *noren*
3. A silk kite
4. Umbrella designed with a crane
5. One thousand origami cranes traditionally given to wish someone well
6. Small figurine of a boy
7. Very old playing cards for the game *Hyakunin Isshu*
8. A traditional eating bowl
9. A fabric covered folder with traditional female figures
10. Traditional teapot and cups with a symbol of happiness
11. Stone ball for a game or exercise
12. Lacquered tray
13. A very old book probably recordings of family names and geneology

FOLK ART FROM MEXICO (page 54 and 55)

1. Tree of Life. This piece depicts animals, Adam and Eve, a heavenly figure, the sun, moon, serpent, and plant life of brilliant colors
2. Gourd decorated as a chicken
3. Chicken napkin holder
4. Black jewelry and figures from Oaxaca region
5. Tarahumara carved wooden figures
6. A santos (saint) figure

7. Ribbon and pompom hat. These hats were worn by men in Chiapas conveying their marital status: if ribbons are loose they are single, if they are tied up they are married
8. A clay bull
9. An indigenous revolutionary doll from Chiapas made in 1994
10. Typical handwoven textiles
11. Wool cross-stitch from Morelia region
12. Lacquerware box